Manufactured–Housing Consumer Finance in the United States

Table of contents

1. Introduction

This white paper provides background on manufactured housing, including the market and regulatory environment, as well as on consumers who purchase or rent manufactured housing. The Consumer Financial Protection Bureau (Bureau) initiated research into manufactured housing to provide the Bureau and others with a more comprehensive understanding of manufactured housing and its financing.

Manufactured housing accounts for six percent of all occupied housing and a much smaller fraction of home loan originations in the U.S. These fractions notwithstanding, manufactured housing is of interest to the Bureau for at least two reasons. First, it is an important source of affordable housing, in particular for rural and low-income consumers. Second, manufactured housing may raise particular consumer protection concerns due to the nature of the retail and financing markets for manufactured housing. This is particularly true to the extent that buyers of manufactured homes are more likely to belong to groups, such as older or lower-income families, that might be considered financially vulnerable.

Compared with site-built housing and mortgage finance generally, data and information on manufactured housing are relatively sparse. Yet, manufactured housing differs from site-built housing in several ways, including housing costs and the market for home financing. A key goal of the white paper is to bring together information and data from a number of data sources, each of which contributes to a more-complete picture of manufactured housing. The Bureau primarily analyzed data such as the American Community Survey (ACS), the American Housing Survey (AHS), data reported under the Home Mortgage Disclosure Act (HMDA), Manufactured Homes Survey (MH Census), and the Survey of Consumer Finances (SCF). The Bureau also analyzed proprietary data voluntarily provided to the CFPB.[1] To complement its analysis of these data sources, the Bureau engaged in outreach to industry groups, consumer groups, government agencies, and a variety of market participants and observers.

Key findings of this white paper include:

- **Manufactured housing is disproportionately located in non-metropolitan areas.** Nationwide, manufactured housing accounts for six percent of occupied housing, compared with fourteen percent of housing located outside of metropolitan areas. At the county level, the share of manufactured housing can reach even greater levels: in 112 U.S. counties—predominately in Southern and Western states—over one-third of homes are manufactured housing.

- **Compared with residents of site-built homes, manufactured-housing residents are somewhat more likely to be older and tend to have lower incomes or net worth.** A greater proportion of households that live in manufactured housing are headed by a retiree (32 percent) than site-built households (24 percent).[2] The median income for households that live in manufactured homes is roughly half the median income among families in other types of homes. The median net worth among households that live in manufactured housing is about one-quarter of the median net worth among other households.

- **Manufactured homes typically cost less than site-built homes.** On a square-foot basis, manufactured homes cost less than half as much as the estimated $94 per square foot for new site-built housing construction in 2013.[3] The average sales price of a new single-section manufactured home was about $43,000 in the first six months of 2014. The average price of a new multi-section manufactured home was about $78,000, though expenses of transport, siting, and construction add-ons can add to the cost. The

---

[1] To preserve the confidentiality of the data providers, the white paper includes only limited discussion of the analyses based on these data and does not identify the institutions that provided the data. Conclusions from the analyses of the proprietary data generally align with the conclusions in this report based on publicly available data sources. The proprietary data contain no direct consumer identifiers.

[2] CFPB analysis of Survey of Consumer Finances (SCF), 2004–2010.

[3] U.S. Census Bureau, *Cost & Size Comparisons: New Manufactured Homes and Single-Family Site-Built Homes (2007 – 2013), available at* https://www.census.gov/construction/mhs/pdf/sitebuiltvsmh.pdf *, data available at* https://www.census.gov/construction/mhs/mhsindex.html. (This survey was sponsored by the U.S. Dep't of Hous. & Urban Dev. (HUD))

most basic single-section homes can sell for less than $20,000, and a larger home with custom designs or optional finishes and features may cost $100,000 or more.

- **About three-fifths of manufactured-housing residents who own their home also own the land it is sited on.** These consumers generally have the option either to title their home as real property and to obtain financing through a real estate mortgage loan or to title the property as personal property and to obtain chattel financing.

- **An estimated 65 percent of borrowers who own their land and who took out a loan to buy a manufactured home between 2001 and 2010 financed the purchase with a chattel loan.** There are tradeoffs between real-property financing and chattel financing. Chattel loans often have lower origination costs and may close more quickly than mortgages (loans secured by real property). Interest rates on chattel loans, however, may be between 50 and 500 basis points more expensive than real property loans, and chattel loans generally have lesser consumer protections than mortgages. The extent to which consumers are aware of these tradeoffs and how consumers weigh them remains an open question.

- **Manufactured-home owners typically pay higher interest rates for their loans than site-built borrowers.** For example, about 68 percent of all manufactured-housing purchase loans (chattel as well as real property loans) reported under the Home Mortgage Disclosure Act in 2012 met the definition of a "higher-priced mortgage loan" (HPML), a definition developed to identify a set of loans that might be considered subprime. By comparison, only three percent of loans for site-built homes were HPMLs. Even within the set of HPMLs, manufactured-home loans tend to have higher rates.

- **The current state of manufactured housing production, retail, and financing reflects in part a rapid growth during the 1990s and subsequent sharp contraction**. In the 1990s credit standards and underwriting practices for manufactured-housing loans became more lax, and the market boomed. The market collapsed, however, in the early 2000s as consumers began experiencing repayment difficulties, and the market significantly contracted. Poor manufactured-home loan quality drove high defaults. For example, in the year 2000 alone, more than 75,000 consumers had their manufactured homes repossessed, about 3.5 times the typical number during the 1990s. Between the beginning of 1999 and the end of 2002, repossessed inventory grew more than fourfold to $1.3 billion. Today, more than a decade after this collapse, production and sales remain at depressed levels, and the secondary market is extremely limited.

These findings underscore the importance of the manufactured housing sector as a source of affordable housing for some consumers, including those outside of metropolitan areas, older households, and lower-income households. At the same time, these same groups include consumers that may be considered more financially vulnerable and, thus, may particularly stand to benefit from strong consumer protections.

The Bureau has recognized that certain provisions of the Dodd-Frank Act that the Bureau implemented through rules that took effect in January, 2014, may affect the market for smaller-size mortgages and, more specifically, the manufactured housing segment of the market, in ways that differ from the rules' effect on other market segments.[4] Because the rules have been effective for only a few months, and because there are lags in the availability of data, it would be premature to reach conclusions on the market-wide effects of the rules.

The Bureau will continue to monitor the effect of its rules on the manufactured housing industry and on consumers who purchase or seek to purchase manufactured homes. As part of this ongoing monitoring, the Bureau will continue to engage with stakeholders and will encourage others to build greater knowledge of the manufactured housing market, the consumers in that market, and the differences between the site-built and manufactured housing markets.

---

[4] *See infra* Appendix for a description of some of these rules.

2. Manufactured housing and its residents

2.1 What is a manufactured home?

Manufactured homes account for a small but important share of single-family housing in the U.S. Manufactured homes are commonly referred to as "mobile homes" or "trailers" but in fact are a specific type of factory-built housing, constructed in accordance with the U.S. Department of Housing and Urban Development's (HUD's) Manufactured Home Construction and Safety Standards code. A factory-built home constructed after June 15, 1976 is eligible for designation as a manufactured home if, among other things, the structure is at least 320 square feet and constructed on a permanent chassis.[5] Homes that meet these criteria are affixed with a HUD label that indicates the homes' compliance with the relevant HUD codes.

Manufactured housing should be distinguished from trailers, RVs, and park-model homes. These vehicles and homes (which are built to different standards than manufactured homes) are generally treated as motor vehicles for legal and financing purposes (though in some cases they may be permanently sited). On the other hand, modular homes—which are often built in the same facilities as manufactured homes—are constructed on site using modular components and are generally treated as real property.

Manufactured homes are available with numerous size and floor-plan options. The homes are built in a factory and then transported by means of the permanent chassis directly to a placement site after purchase or to retail centers. Single-section homes may be transported in a

---

[5] 42 U.S.C. §5402.

single piece, whereas multi-section homes are transported in multiple pieces that are joined on site. In 2013, single-section homes accounted for 46 percent of manufactured home placements, and this share has fluctuated between one-quarter and over one-half since the early 1990s. Manufactured homes are required to be professionally installed in accordance with HUD's installation standards.[6]

Manufactured homes may be placed on individual land plots that are owned by the manufactured-home owner, or the homes may be placed on rented land, including on leased lots within manufactured home communities. Manufactured housing communities generally require a homeowner or renter to pay ground rent and additional fees for shared amenities, services, and utilities. Some communities are age-restricted and function as retirement or seasonal homes for residents aged 55 or older. Historically, around 25–30 percent of manufactured homes have been placed within manufactured housing communities, though the share of new homes placed in communities has grown in recent years.[7]

The bulk of a manufactured home's appreciation potential comes from the land on which it sits, not the structure itself, so the most important factor determining the appreciation (or depreciation) of manufactured housing is generally land ownership.[8] However, manufactured-home owners that own the land under the home may still not enjoy appreciation in the property's value if the structure depreciates more quickly than the land increases in value. Thus, whether a manufactured-home owner realizes appreciation can depend on a number of factors beyond land ownership including the home's size, location, and investment in maintenance and upkeep.[9]

Once placed, manufactured homes are typically not moved from their original site. Site installation includes settlement upon a permanent or semi-permanent foundation support. Foundation types range from insulated basements to concrete slabs to block, anchor, and strap

---

[6] *See* 24 CFR part 3285.

[7] *See supra* note3.

[8] Kevin Jewell, Consumers Union, *Manufactured Housing Appreciation: Stereotypes and Data* (Apr. 2003) *available at* http://consumersunion.org/pdf/mh/Appreciation.pdf.

[9] Note that the appraisal process for manufactured homes often differs from the process for site-built homes. In particular, manufactured homes titled as chattel are often appraised using "blue book" type of valuation: a published guide that provides a value for the house based on the model, the year manufactured, and the condition of the house. If a more traditional appraisal is done (generally only for a manufactured home affixed to land), then sometimes only other manufactured homes may be used as comparables. Availability of comparables, therefore, may also affect valuation of manufactured homes, especially in low-density areas.

fixtures. Even manufactured homes secured by semi-permanent foundations, however, are infrequently moved. As of 2011, the vast majority of owner-occupied manufactured homes in the U.S. were on the same site upon which they were first placed.[10] About two-thirds of owner-occupied manufactured homes that are moved from their original site have been re-sold, and about one-third remain in the possession of their original residents.[11]

An important difference between manufactured homes and site-built homes is their potentially differing legal treatment. Titling a manufactured home as real property is a choice in most states if the owner permanently affixes the manufactured home to land they own (or rented land with a sufficiently lengthy lease). However, even where the manufactured home is permanently affixed to land, the owner has the option to title the home as personal property (chattel). About three-quarters of states have statutorily-defined processes for converting a manufactured home's title from personal property to real property.[12] Generally, manufactured homes are treated as personal property by default, and documentation that the home has become a fixture is required to be considered real property. As discussed in Section 2.5, the decision whether to title a manufactured home as real or personal property affects property taxation, applicability of consumer protection laws, and financing options.

2.2 Geographic distribution of manufactured housing

Manufactured homes account for about six percent of all occupied U.S. housing. As shown in Figure 1, manufactured housing is more common in Southern and Western states, where manufactured homes account for as much as 17 percent of total housing stock (in South

---

[10] According to US Census Bureau American Housing Survey (AHS), 2011, more than 80 percent of owner-occupied manufactured homes in the US remain on the site where they were first placed. This estimate excludes the roughly eight percent of responses that were "don't know" or "not reported." Including these responses reduces the estimated fraction of homes that remain on the same site to about 75 percent. U.S. Census Bureau, *American Housing Survey for the United States (AHS): 2011*, Table C-01-AH, pg., 4, *available at* http://www.census.gov/content/dam/Census/programs-surveys/ahs/data/2011/h150-11.pdf (CFPB analysis of US Census Bureau American Housing Survey (AHS) microdata, 2011).

[11] *Id.*

[12] *See* Corporation for Enterprise Development (CFED) & National Consumer Law Center (NCLC), *Titling Homes as Real Property* (2009), *available at* http://cfed.org/assets/pdfs/mh_realproperty.pdf.

Carolina). Manufactured housing is less common in several Northeastern states. At the county level, the share of manufactured housing can reach even greater levels: in 112 U.S. counties—predominately in southeastern and southwestern states—over one-third of homes are manufactured housing (Figure 2).

Manufactured housing is more prevalent in rural areas. About two-thirds of all occupied manufactured homes in the U.S. are located outside of metropolitan statistical areas (MSAs), and 14 percent of homes in non-MSA counties are manufactured homes.[13]

Manufactured housing industry participants indicate that the greater share of manufactured housing in rural areas may be due to a number of factors including low population density, which may limit scale efficiencies for residential construction, and in some cases higher transportation costs for materials to construct site-built homes. Industry participants also frequently point to zoning restrictions as an important reason for the lower prevalence of manufactured housing in metropolitan areas. Local zoning laws, particularly in and around large cities, commonly preclude placement of manufactured homes as dwellings. For example, a city might require that a home be at least 20 feet wide, thereby precluding siting a single-section manufactured home, and foundation requirements may discourage placement of manufactured housing.[14] In some areas, manufactured homes are allowed only in specifically designated areas, such as specifically zoned communities or subdivisions. Restrictive zoning and prohibitive land development costs are among the reasons there has not been significant development of new manufactured home communities in the past decade, though recent trends indicate that investment in existing communities is increasing.[15]

---

[13] US Census Bureau American Community Survey (ACS), 2008-2012, *available at* http://www.census.gov/acs/www/data_documentation/data_main/.

[14] Ronald A. Wirtz, Fed. Res. Bank of Minneapolis, *Hello, have we met? Manufactured Housing Suffers an Image Problem* (fedgazette July 1, 2005), *available at* http://www.minneapolisfed.org/research/pub_display.cfm?id=1484.

[15] Multifamily manufactured housing community securities' share of CMBS issuance has grown to about four percent in the past decade. Additionally, in April 2014, Freddie Mac announced a program for manufactured housing community loan securitization. *See* Al Yoon, *Freddie Mac Moves Into the Trailer Park*, Wall Street Journal, April 30, 2014 *available at* http://online.wsj.com/news/articles/SB10001424052702303948104579534120298682710. *See also* Gary Rivlin, *The Cold, Hard Lessons of Mobile Home U*, New York Times Magazine, March 13 2014, *available at* http://www.nytimes.com/2014/03/16/magazine/the-cold-hard-lessons-of-mobile-home-u.html; and L.A. "Tony" Kovach, *Sensationalistic 'Cold Hard Lessons of Mobil Home U" New York Times Article by Gary Rivlin Draws Manufactured Home Industry Ire, Desire, and Fire*, Manufactured Home Living News (2014), *available at* http://manufacturedhomelivingnews.com/sensationalistic-cold-hard-lessons-of-mobile-home-u-new-york-times-

FIGURE 1: MANUFACTURED HOUSING SHARE OF OCCUPIED HOUSING UNITS, BY STATE.[16]

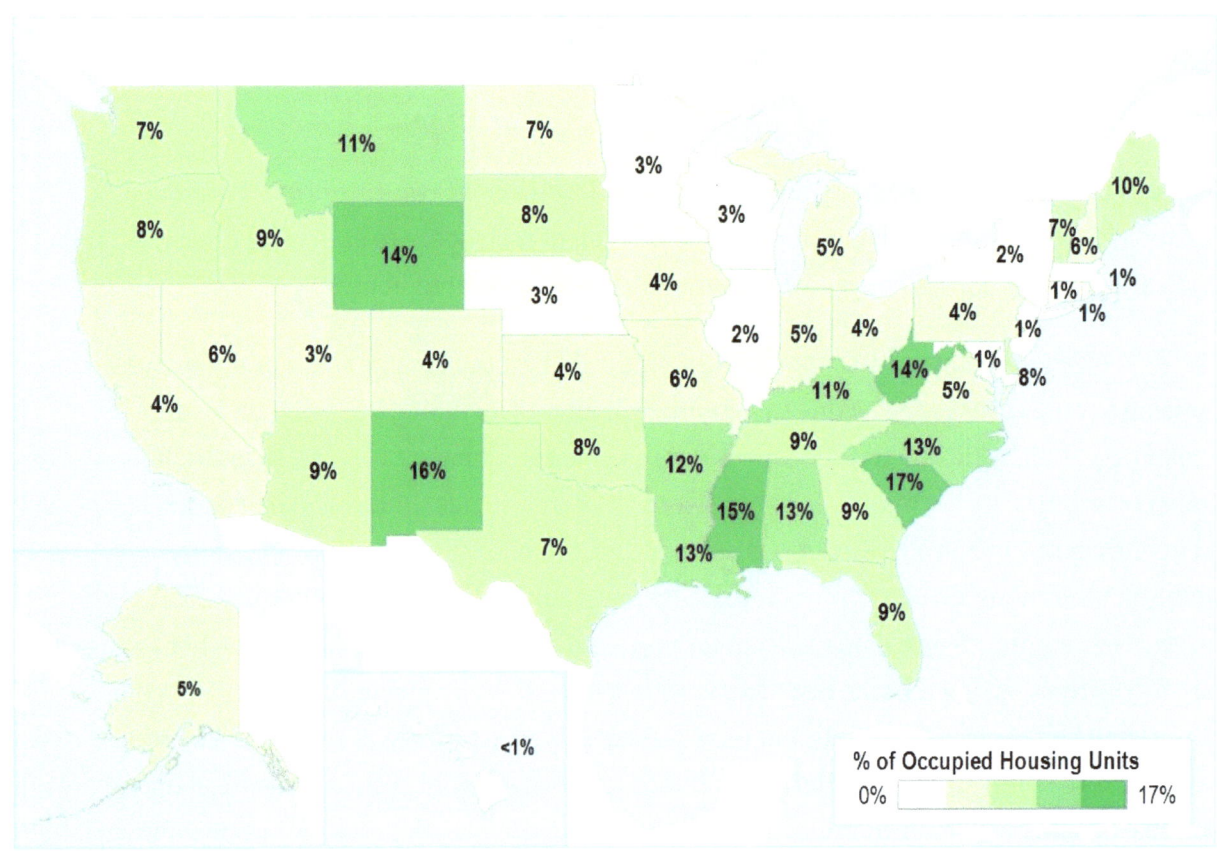

article-by-gary-rivlin-draws-manufactured home-industry-ire-desire-and-fire/ (discussion of growing investments in existing manufactured housing communities).

[16] US Census Bureau ACS, *supra* note 13. Similar results hold for manufactured housing as a proportion of all housing stock.

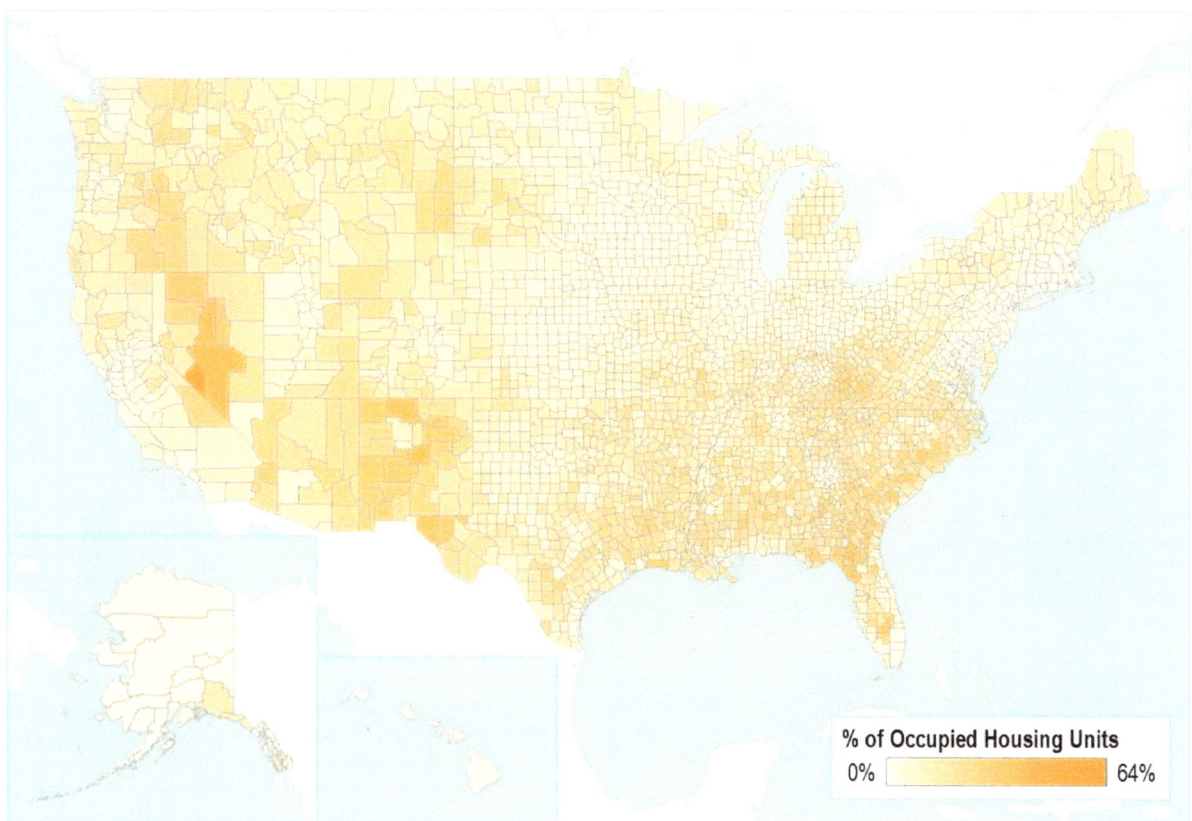

% of Occupied Housing Units
0% — 64%

2.3   Residents of manufactured housing

Certain consumer segments are disproportionately represented among owners and renters of manufactured homes, in particular older consumers, consumers that have completed only high school, households with relatively low income, and households with relatively low net worth. As shown in the top panel of Figure 3, among owner-occupant households, the heads of households that lived in manufactured housing are a bit more likely to be younger than 30 or older than 70 than are site-built owner-occupant household heads. The median age of a head-of-household owner of a manufactured home is 53 years, identical to the median owner-occupant head-of-household for all home types.[18] The bottom panel of Figure 3 shows that for renters with a head

---

[17] US Census Bureau ACS, *supra* note 13.
[18] *Id.*

between the ages of 30 and 59, a greater share rented a manufactured home than a site-built home.

Nearly one-fifth of households that live in manufactured homes have an older (55 or older) single head of household with no children in the home, compared with less than 15 percent of households that live in site-built homes.[19] A greater proportion of households that live in manufactured housing are headed by a retiree (32 percent) than site-built households (24 percent).[20]

---

[19] CFPB analysis of Survey of Consumer Finances (SCF), *supra* note 2.
[20] *Id.*

FIGURE 3:   HEAD-OF-HOUSEHOLD AGE DISTRIBUTION[21]

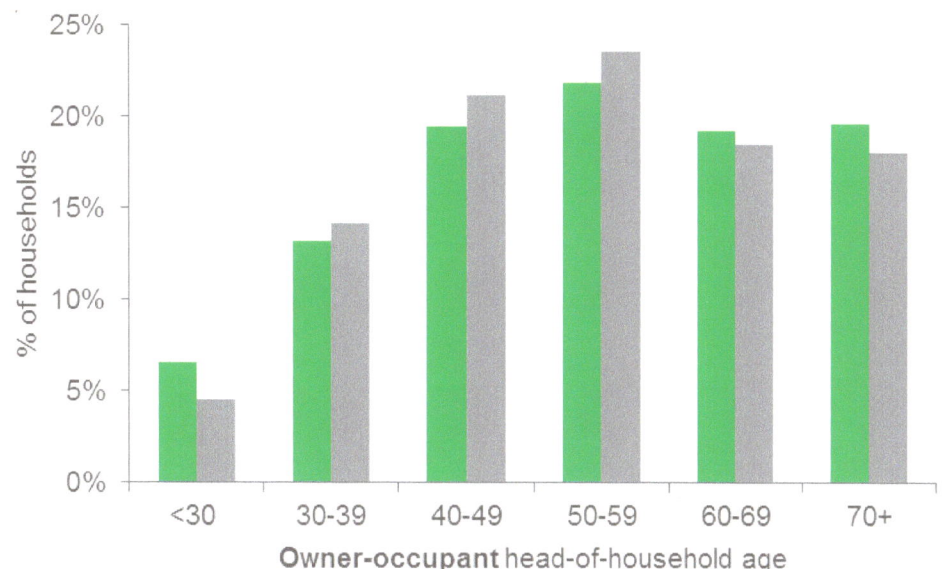

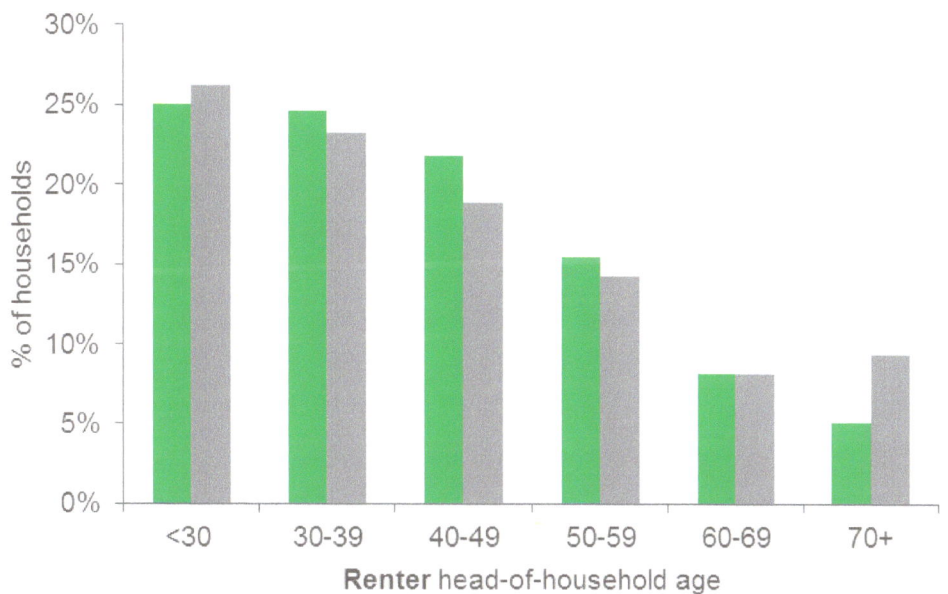

■ Manufactured housing   ■ Site-built housing

---

[21] US Census Bureau ACS, *supra* note 13.

As shown in Table 1, manufactured-home buyers tend to be older at the time of purchase than site-built buyers, with a difference in the median age of five years (42 years compared with 37 years). This age difference is narrower among first-time homebuyers and is wider for repeat homebuyers.

TABLE 1: MEDIAN AGE OF HOUSEHOLD HEAD AT PURCHASE[22]

	All buyers	First-time homebuyers	Repeat buyers
Site-built housing	37	31	41
Manufactured housing	42	33	49

There is significant mobility from site-built housing into manufactured homes—most recent purchasers of manufactured homes moved from site-built houses or apartments (where they may have previously rented or owned). However, manufactured-home owners are much more likely than site-built owners to have moved from another manufactured home. About 20 percent of households who recently purchased a manufactured home moved in from a previous manufactured home residence.

Adult residents of owner-occupied manufactured housing tend to have lower levels of educational attainment, on average, than adult residents in site-built housing (see Table 2). Differences in the distributions of income for home buyers by the type of structure (manufactured or site-built) may in part reflect these differences in educational attainment. HMDA data for borrowers with purchase-money mortgages taken out in 2012 show that households that financed the purchase of manufactured housing had lower incomes on average than those who financed the purchase of site-built housing (see Figure 4).[23] The percentage of purchasers with incomes below $35,000 is higher for manufactured housing than for site-built housing.

---

[22] U.S. Census Bureau AHS, *supra* note10.

[23] Bureau of Consumer Fin. Prot, *Home Mortgage Disclosure Act (HMDA) Data 2012,* available at http://www.consumerfinance.gov/hmda/. The analysis is restricted to only loans secured by an owner-occupied, 1–4 family property and excludes loans taken out by a business.

TABLE 2: HIGHEST LEVEL OF EDUCATIONAL ATTAINMENT BY RESIDENTS AGES 25 OR OLDER IN OWNER-OCCUPIED HOUSEHOLDS[24]

	High school or less	Some college	College degree or above
Site-built residents	37%	21%	42%
Manufactured-housing residents	67%	20%	13%

FIGURE 4: BORROWER INCOME[25]

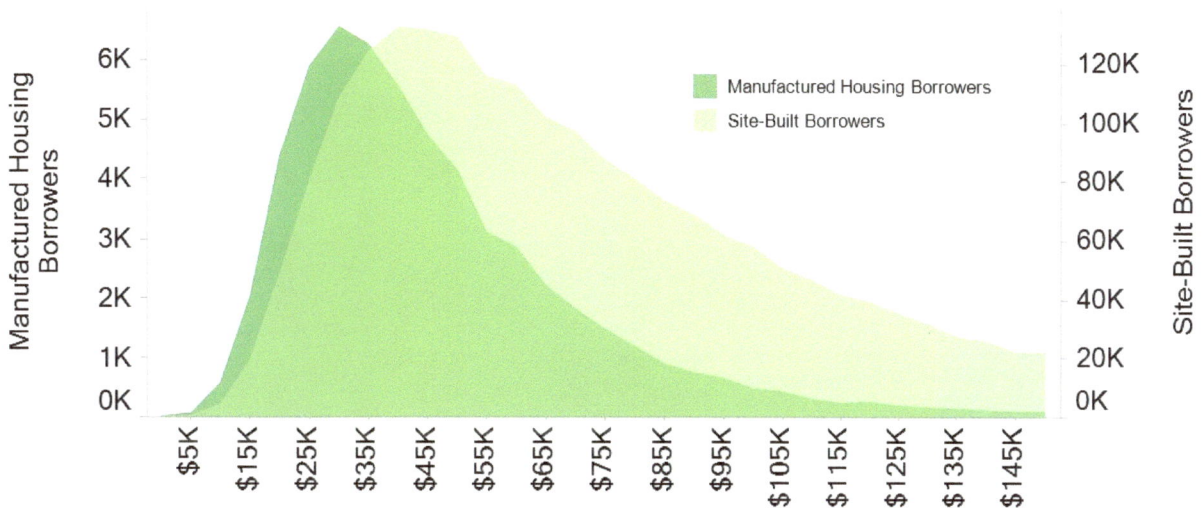

Manufactured-home residents have lower net worth, assets, and debt than other families. The 2004–2010 Surveys of Consumer Finances indicate that the median net worth among households that lived in manufactured housing of $26,000 (in 2010 dollars) was just about one-quarter the median net worth of families in site-built homes (Table 3).[26] The difference in income by type of home for purchase-money borrowers shown in Figure 4 holds more generally for all families: median income for families that live in manufactured homes is a bit more than $26,000 per year, or roughly half the median income for other families. Families in

---

[24] US Census Bureau ACS, *supra* note13. Note that tables include all residents of owner-occupied housing units.
[25] HMDA 2012, *supra* note23.
[26] CFPB analysis of Survey of Consumer Finances (SCF), *supra* note 2.

manufactured homes likewise have lower median assets (about $45,000 compared with $213,000 for families in site-built homes) and median debts ($5,000 compared with $30,000 for families in site-built homes). The median ratio of debts to assets, or leverage ratio, is lower for manufactured-home residents (15 percent) than for other families (22 percent).

	Site-built home	Manufactured home
Median net worth (thous. of 2010 dollars)	112.5	26.0
Median annual income (thous. of 2010 dollars)	50.6	26.4
Median assets (thous. of 2010 dollars)	213.2	44.7
Median debt (thous. of 2010 dollars)	30.3	5.0
Median debt-to-asset ratio (percent)	22.1	15.4

Finally, the racial and ethnic profile of manufactured housing residents differs somewhat from the profile for those who live in site-built homes. The share of non-Hispanic whites, for example, is about seven percentage points greater among those who live in manufactured homes than among families in site-built homes (Table 4). Individuals of Hispanic or Latino ethnicity and those with American Indian or Native Alaskan racial backgrounds make up a greater share of manufactured-home residents than site-built home residents. On the other hand, African Americans and Asians account for a smaller fraction of manufactured-home residents than of site-built residents.

---

[27] CFPB analysis of Survey of Consumer Finances (SCF), *supra* note 2. Figures are in 2010 dollars.

TABLE 4: RACE AND ETHNICITY DISTRIBUTION FOR US RESIDENTS OF SITE-BUILT HOUSING AND MANUFACTURED HOUSING[28]

Ethnicity/Race	Site-built housing residents	Manufactured-housing residents
Hispanic or Latino	16.4%	18.2%
Not Hispanic or Latino	83.6%	81.8%
Non-Hispanic White	63.5%	69.1%
One Race		
White	74.0%	81.3%
Black or African American	12.5%	8.7%
American Indian and Alaska Native	0.8%	1.8%
Asian	5.1%	0.8%
Native Hawaiian and Other Pacific Islander	0.2%	0.1%
Some Other Race	4.8%	5.2%
Two or More Races	2.7%	2.2%

2.4   Housing costs

Manufactured homes typically cost less than site-built homes, both on a square-foot basis and in total. Manufactured homes cost less than half as much as the estimated $94 per square foot for new site-built housing construction in 2013.[29] The average consumer sales price for a new single-section manufactured home was about $43,000 in the first six months of 2014, and the average price of a new multi-section manufactured home was about $78,000.[30] Custom designs or optional finishes and features can raise a home's price tag to $100,000 or more. At the lower-end of the price spectrum, the most basic single-section homes can sell for less than $20,000.

---

[28] US Census Bureau ACS, *supra* note13.

[29] MH Census, *supra* note 3.

[30] MH Census, *supra* note 3.

Transport, siting, and construction represent additional upfront costs to the buyer of a new manufactured home. Initial set-up costs depend on the physical conditions of the site. Installation add-ons such as steps, air conditioning, or patios may increase the price of the home by as much as 25 percent. Moreover, electing to site the home on a permanent foundation can cost an additional $2,000–$10,000.[31] The median combined value of manufactured homes and associated land (among households that own the home and the land) is about 42 percent of the median value of existing site-built homes in the U.S.[32]

Consumers may face different costs depending on whether they own or rent the land. About 48 percent of households that live in manufactured homes own both the home and the land it is placed on, about 30 percent rent the land but own the home, and about 18 percent rent both the site and land.[33] Nationwide, ground rents in non-age-restricted manufactured home communities averaged $393 per month as of late 2013.[34] Even taking into account the additional cost for ground rent particular to some owners of manufactured housing, the ownership costs of manufactured housing are lower than an average site-built home in metro and non-metro areas (see Table 5). Typical all-in housing costs for manufactured-home owners in non-metropolitan areas were over a third less than the costs for households that owned a site-built home in a non-metro area ($608 compared with $948), and the gap is even wider for those residing within metro areas. The monthly cost differences between manufactured and site-built housing were narrower among renters in general, and in particular in non-metropolitan areas, where monthly rents for manufactured homes were about $100 less than rents for site-built properties ($654 compared with $551).[35]

---

[31]Costs may vary based on geographic requirements. Cost estimates provided by various industry participants through CFPB outreach.

[32] US Census Bureau AHS, *supra* note 10.

[33] *Id.*

[34] Press release, John M. Turzer, JLT & Associates, *National Manufactured Home Community Rent Survey Summaries*, (July 2013), *available at* http://jlt-associates.com/uploads/2013_12_National_Survey_Summary_Press_Release_July_2013.pdf.

[35] US Census Bureau AHS, *supra* note 10. For this calculation, site-built units include single-family detached, single-family attached units (e.g., duplexes and townhomes), and multi-family properties such as condominiums and co-operatives. Rental units are defined as both single-family homes and multi-family units, such as apartments, for lease.

TABLE 5: AVERAGE MONTHLY ALL-IN HOUSING COSTS [36]

	Metro		Non-metro	
	Site-built	Manufactured	Site-built	Manufactured
Owner-occupants	$1,505	$686	$948	$608
Renters	$992	$676	$654	$551

Some households may prefer manufactured housing over site-built housing because of its cost, construction speed, architecture and layout, or other factors. In many areas of the country, the decision to live in manufactured housing may also be influenced by the breadth of housing options available in the area, especially in less densely-populated regions. However, data from the American Housing Survey and American Community Survey do not offer clear support for the conjecture that manufactured housing is particularly prevalent in areas with limited affordable site-built or rental housing. More specifically, a comparison of the prevalence of occupied manufactured homes in U.S. counties and various available measures of local affordable housing availability shows no clear correlation between housing availability and the proportion of households that live in manufactured homes. [37]

There is evidence that some households who move into manufactured housing are less satisfied with their homes than those who choose to move into site-built housing. These results suggest that for at least some households, the choice to live in a manufactured home may be more cost-driven than quality-driven. In a nationally representative survey of recent movers, those who moved into manufactured housing were significantly more likely to rate their new house as

---

[36] US Census Bureau AHS, *supra* note 10. Housing tenure refers to the housing unit, so manufactured home owners who rent their site are classified as owner-occupants.

[37] For instance, based on CFPB analysis of ACS data (2008-2012), the share of vacant homes (both manufactured homes and site-built) is 14 percent in counties where occupied manufactured housing is least prevalent and 22 percent in counties where occupied manufactured housing is most prevalent. However, the vacant-for-sale and vacant-for-rent rates are about the same across such counties where manufactured housing is more or less prevalent. In addition, site-built homes are not significantly more expensive in counties where manufactured housing is more prevalent. In counties where manufactured housing is highly prevalent, home values and rents overall tend to be lower. A similar result holds when analysis is restricted to non-MSA counties.

"worse [than their previous residence]" than similarly situated households who moved into site-built housing.[38] This finding is true of lower-income (below 150 percent of the area poverty line) manufactured-housing owners in metro areas and for lower-income manufactured-housing owners who previously rented. However, for owner-occupant households in rural areas and those who had previously owned a home, those moving into manufactured homes were not significantly more likely to report their new residences as "worse."

2.5 The legal treatment of manufactured housing

As noted above, manufactured homes may be titled as either personal or real property. In most cases, re-titling of the home as real estate requires that the home must be affixed to a permanent foundation on land that is owned by the home's owner. The process generally involves surrendering the original title and providing additional documentation to a county land recorder that the home has become a real estate fixture. Since 2004, about one-quarter of new manufactured homes were titled as real estate, though in recent years this proportion has decreased; in 2013 only 14 percent of new manufactured homes were titled as real property.[39] In Texas, which received more than 20 percent of all new manufactured homes shipped in 2013, about 10 percent of all new manufactured homes and only seven percent of used manufactured homes purchased in 2013 from retailers were titled as real property.[40]

The way in which a manufactured home is titled affects property taxation, applicability of consumer protection laws, and financing options.[41] To qualify for mortgage financing, a consumer must title the manufactured home as real property and encumber both the land and

---

[38] US Census Bureau AHS, *supra* note 10.

[39] MH Census, *supra* note 3.

[40] Manufactured Housing Institute, *Manufactured Home Shipments by State (1990 - 2013), available at* https://www.manufacturedhousing.org/admin/template/subbrochures/390temp.pdf (Data source: Institute for Building Technology and Safety (IBTS)); Texas Manufactured Housing Association, Stats: Payment Types for Retail Sales, *available* at http://www.texasmha.com/industry-resources/stats/payment-types-for-retail-sales.

[41] For a discussion of state and federal laws' applicability to manufactured homes titled as real or personal property, *see CFED & NCLC, supra* note 12. *See also* Government Accountability Office (GAO), GAO-07-879, *Federal Housing Administration, Agency Should Assess the Effects of Proposed Changes to the Manufactured Home Loan Program* (Aug. 2007), *available at* http://www.gao.gov/new.items/d07879.pdf.

home; otherwise, the consumer can obtain only a chattel loan with the lender taking a security interest in the manufactured home.[42] For this reason, manufactured homes in land-lease communities —about 30 percent of all manufactured housing placements in recent years—are generally only eligible for chattel financing.[43]

There are material differences between mortgage financing for manufactured homes and chattel financing. To begin with, chattel loans may be priced between 50 and 500 basis points higher, all else equal, than a comparable mortgage loan for a manufactured home.[44] Additionally, chattel loans are also generally for shorter loan terms which affect the monthly costs. On the other hand, mortgages for manufactured homes generally have higher costs at origination relative to chattel loans (including the cost of recording the mortgage) and generally take longer to close than chattel loans. In addition, mortgage loans encumber the land as well as the manufactured home whereas the chattel loan gives the lender a security interest only in the home. Furthermore, there are specific consumer protection laws that apply only to mortgage financing, including parts of the Real Estate Settlement Procedures Act (RESPA) and various state foreclosure and repossession laws. Thus, manufactured-home owners who can choose either chattel or mortgage financing (generally, those who own the land to which the manufactured home is being permanently affixed) may face a tradeoff between lower costs at origination and a quicker closing with less collateral, on the one hand, and lower total costs over the life of the loan along with greater consumer protections on the other.

As previously noted, the vast majority of manufactured housing stock is titled as chattel and thus eligible only for chattel financing. The Bureau estimates that approximately three-quarters of all manufactured-home owners with purchase financing take out a chattel loan. According to 2011 AHS data, about 60 percent of manufactured-home owners who own their home also own the land. Among consumers who purchased their home between 2001 and 2010, about 51 percent owned the land. We estimate based on AHS data that 65 percent or more of land-

---

[42] In discussing loans for manufactured housing, the term "mortgage" is often used as shorthand for real property loans (as opposed to chattel loans).

[43] MH Census, *supra* note 3. Anecdotal evidence and American Housing Survey (AHS) data suggest that an even greater share, potentially almost half, of the stock of manufactured homes purchased in recent years are located in communities.

[44] *See* Wirtz, *supra* note 14; industry outreach.

owning consumers who took out a home-purchase loan between 2001 and 2010 had a chattel loan.[45]

The extent to which consumers are aware of theses tradeoffs and how consumers weigh them remains an open question. It is not clear to what degree upfront costs and convenience, lack of availability for mortgage financing, or lack of relevant information about financing options drive consumers to chattel financing. Some consumers may not wish to encumber their land in a mortgage transaction for reasons other than upfront cost or time, especially if the land is owned free and clear or would require partition.

---

[45] US Census Bureau AHS, *supra* note 10.

3. Production, sales, and financing

3.1 Historical manufactured housing finance market dynamics

Production of manufactured homes increased steadily in the mid-1990s but dropped sharply in the late 1990s into the early 2000s. In only four years, annual new manufactured home factory shipments dropped to less than half the peak of nearly 375,000 in 1998, to about 170,000 in 2002. In the late 1990s, a market rapidly grew to finance loans for these homes and securitize the underlying manufactured-home loan assets (see Figure 5). The sharp and sustained decline in manufactured home purchases after 1998 was driven to a large extent by the collapse of the secondary market for manufactured-housing loans after market participants suffered sharp losses on securities backed by manufactured-housing loans.[46]

The manufactured housing crisis was precipitated by behavior similar to that which led to the larger subprime and "Alt-A" housing market collapse and financial crisis less than a decade later. Manufactured home lending standards, for example, relaxed through the late 1990s as lenders provided financing to less creditworthy borrowers. In order to generate origination volume, creditors lowered borrower credit standards and documentation requirements. To make monthly payments more affordable and qualify more buyers, lenders lengthened loan

---

[46] The declining number of shipments and placements might in part reflect slackened demand for manufactured homes to the extent that financing for site-built homes became more available during the early 2000s and, consequently, buyers that otherwise might have purchased an manufactured home instead purchased a site-built home.

terms. Borrowers from Green Tree Financial, once the largest manufactured-housing lender, experienced an increase in average loan terms to 25 years in 1997 from just 13 years in 1987.[47] As a result, consumers with longer-term loans built less equity in their homes as principal payments were spread over a longer period. Moreover, retailer fraud in the form of artificially inflated home appraisals and invoice prices or falsified credit applications was a recognized issue as home sales surged.[48]

FIGURE 5: MANUFACTURED-HOUSING LOAN-BACKED ABS ISSUANCE AND NEW MANUFACTURED HOME SHIPMENTS[49]

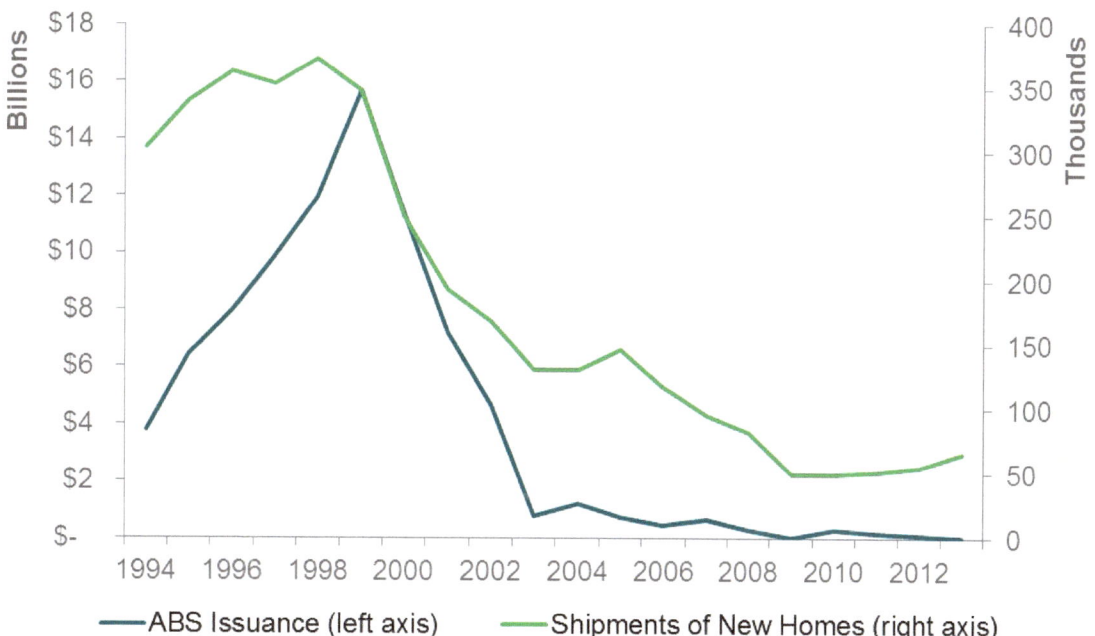

The poor quality of many loans for manufactured housing led to high rates of defaults and repossessions in the early 2000s. Many consumers who had financed the purchase of a manufactured home throughout the late 1990s and early 2000s had difficulty making payments. The FHA Title I portfolio saw default rates between 30 and 54 percent on loan vintages

---

[47] Alex Berenson, *A Boom Built Upon Sand, Gone Bust*, N.Y. Times, November 25, 2001, *available at* http://www.nytimes.com/2001/11/25/business/a-boom-built-upon-sand-gone-bust.html?pagewanted=2&pagewanted=all.

[48] Standard & Poor's, *Manufactured Housing Criteria* (Jan., 2000) *available at* http://www.securitization.net/pdf/mh99web.pdf.

[49] Asset-Backed Alert, ABAlert.com, 2014; MH Census, *supra* note 3.

originated between 1995 and 2002 (as of 2007), and the highest rate of payment defaults came within the first three to five years of a loan's repayment. [50] In the year 2000 alone, over 75,000 consumers had their homes repossessed, whereas a rate of 20,000 repossessions annually was the norm throughout boom years. [51] By the end of 2002, repossessed inventory had grown more than fourfold since the beginning of 1999 to $1.3 billion. [52]

As the manufactured housing boom fell from its peak between late 1998 and early 2002, at least eight sizable market lenders exited the market. Conseco, Inc., filed for bankruptcy in 2002, four years after merging with Green Tree Financial. As the largest manufactured-housing lender with 54 percent of originations in 2000, Conseco's bankruptcy reflected the industry-wide trend of deteriorating loan quality and drove losses in the secondary market.

As issuers and purchasers of manufactured housing asset backed securities, including chattel, the GSEs sustained large losses within their manufactured housing portfolios. As of 1999, Fannie Mae had captured about 24 percent of the overall manufactured housing market and subsequently aimed to increase manufactured housing purchases, as one way to meet affordable-housing goals. [53] Loan vintages from 1999 and later proved to be the worst performing as delinquencies and defaults rose well into the next decade. [54] Moreover, troubled assets represented a significant portion of the GSEs' manufactured housing portfolio—as of October, 2002 Conseco securities represented 70 percent of Fannie Mae's manufactured housing balances. [55]

---

[50] GAO, *supra* note 41.

[51] Berenson, *supra* note 47; Daniel Guido, *Manufactured Mess*, *Builder*, (Oct., 2001), *available at* http://www.builderonline.com/mortgages-and-banking/manufactured-mess.aspx?dfpzone=magazines.archive.

[52] Wirtz, *supra* note 14.

[53] Fannie Mae internal memorandum, "HUD Housing Goals Options," June 15, 1999. *available at* http://fcic-static.law.stanford.edu/cdn_media/fcic-docs/1999-06-15%20Fannie%20Memo%20re%20HUD%20Housing%20Goals%20Options.pdf (Memorandum is available in the Financial Crisis Inquiry Commission Archives).

[54] JPMorgan Global Structured Finance Research, "ABS Performance Statistics," September 25, 2002. *Available at* http://www.securitization.net/pdf/jp_stats_090102.pdf; Wachovia Securities, "Manufactured Housing Loss Severities Remain Stubbornly High," February 12, 2002. *Available at* http://www.securitization.net/pdf/wachovia_loss_021202.pdf.

[55] Fannie Mae internal presentation, "Conseco Manufactured Housing Business Data Gaps Lessons Learned," March 24, 2003, *available at* http://fcic-static.law.stanford.edu/cdn_media/fcic-docs/2003-03-24%20Fannie%20Mae%20Conseco%20Manufactured%20Housing%20Business-%20Data%20Gaps%20Lessons%20Learned.pdf

Many securities backed by manufactured-housing loans were considered to be high credit quality by the ratings agencies when the securities were issued and, in turn, by the GSEs that relied upon the rating agencies' assessments.[56] This proved problematic as issuances were downgraded through the manufactured housing crisis. Freddie Mac halted purchases of manufactured housing securities after 2002. In 2002, all of Freddie Mac's portfolio of manufactured housing securities were rated BBB or above; by 2004 over half were rated below BBB- .[57] Similarly, 99 percent of Fannie Mae's guaranteed and portfolio manufactured-housing-backed securities were considered investment grade in mid-2003, and this figure dropped to three-quarters by mid-2004.[58] In mid-2003 Fannie Mae owned or guaranteed $9.1 billion in manufactured-housing securities, and by the end of 2004, after substantial impairments, the portfolio was valued at just $5.4 billion.[59] Issuance of securities backed by manufactured-housing loans rapidly declined since its peak and has not returned to any great extent since the precipitous crash.

3.2   Size and composition of the financing market for manufactured housing

HMDA data from 2012 indicate that loans for manufactured housing represented 2.5 percent of all first-lien home-purchase transactions to owner-occupants.[60] This figure is likely an underestimate of the proportion of manufactured housing finance transactions, given the

---

[56] *See, e.g.,* Fannie Mae, *Conseco Manufactured Housing Business Data Gaps Lessons Learned* (Mar. 24 2003), available at http://fcic-static.law.stanford.edu/cdn_media/fcic-docs/2003-03-24%20Fannie%20Mae%20Conseco%20Manufactured%20Housing%20Business-%20Data%20Gaps%20Lessons%20Learned.pdf (presentation related that Fannie Mae "relied completely on one reference point, the rating agencies" with respect to manufactured housing risk) (available in Financial Crisis Inquiry Commission Archives).

[57] Freddie Mac Annual Reports, 2003-2004. *Available at* http://www.freddiemac.com/investors/ar/pdf/2004annualrpt.pdf ; http://www.freddiemac.com/investors/ar/pdf/2003annualrpt.pdf

[58] Fannie Mae, *Form 10-Q, Quarter ending June 31, 2003*; Fannie Mae, *Form 10-Q, Quarter ending June 30, 2004, available at* http://www.fanniemae.com/portal/about-us/investor-relations/sec-filings.html.

[59] Fannie Mae, *Form 10-Q: Quarter ending June 31, 2003, available at* http://www.fanniemae.com/resources/file/ir/pdf/quarterly-annual-results/2004/2004_form10K.pdf

[60] HMDA 2012, *supra* 23. The analysis is restricted to only loans secured by an owner-occupied, 1–4 family property and excludes loans taken out by a business.

current reporting requirements for the data.[61] More than 2,000 institutions reported originating one or more manufactured housing purchase loans in 2012. HMDA requires data collection for dwelling-secured loans made by certain creditors. Loans reported in HMDA include both chattel and mortgage loans, but it is not possible to definitively distinguish between these types of collateral in the HMDA data.

Because manufactured housing lending may be considered by some lenders to be a specialty niche, many mortgage lenders do not originate chattel loans. Based on conversations with industry participants, it appears that the national lending market for chattel loans is concentrated among five lenders: 21st Mortgage, Vanderbilt Mortgage, Triad Financial Services, U.S. Bank, and San Antonio Federal Credit Union.[62] These national chattel lenders accounted for over 52 percent of the manufactured-home purchase-money mortgages reported in the 2012 HMDA data. This likely understates these institutions' share of the chattel market, as HMDA captures both mortgages and chattel loans. For smaller manufactured-housing loans ($50,000 or less), these lenders represent over three-fifths of HMDA purchase-loan transactions. Other chattel lenders include smaller regional or community-based institutions, so the number of lenders serving local markets varies.

Manufactured-housing loans are typically smaller than loans for site-built housing. As shown in Figure 6, most manufactured-housing purchasers finance between $10,000 and $80,000. The median loan amount for site-built home purchase was $176,000, more than three times the manufactured home purchase loan median of $55,000. Some of the variability of loan balances for manufactured homes comes from the fact that many of the manufactured-housing loans are home only, and the loans for site-built properties are for both home and site. Unfortunately the HMDA data do not identify loans secured only by the home or by the home and land. Based on survey data of consumers, the average manufactured-home buyer who financed a purchase

---

[61]HMDA likely underreports portions of the manufactured housing lending market since manufactured housing is especially prevalent in rural America. Small depository institutions (DIs) and those exclusively in non-metropolitan areas are not required to report data for HMDA. Similarly, non-DIs with fewer than 100 purchase-money or refinance loans or less than five applications, originations, or purchased loans from metropolitan areas are not required to report.

[62] 21st Mortgage and Vanderbilt Mortgage are wholly owned subsidiaries of Clayton Homes, a Berkshire Hathaway corporation and the nation's largest manufactured housing producer. Triad Financial Services did not report HMDA data for the years analyzed in this publication. Another originator with a large share of manufactured-housing loans, Wells Fargo, engages primarily in real estate-secured lending for manufactured homes.

between 2006 and 2010 obtained a purchase loan for $31,000 if they bought the home and not the land, and $65,000 if they also owned the land.[63]

FIGURE 6: LOAN AMOUNT DISTRIBUTION, HOME PURCHASE LOANS FOR MANUFACTURED AND SITE-BUILT HOMES[64]

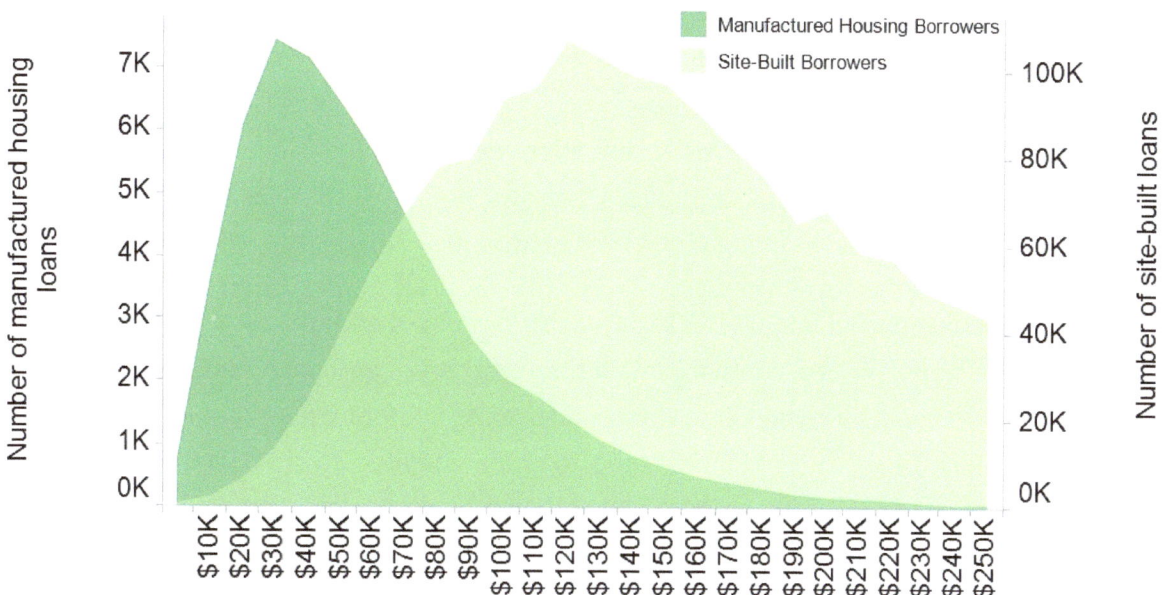

[63] US Census Bureau AHS, *supra* note 10. Available data does not allow analysis of landowning consumers who financed their home only versus land and home together.

[64] HMDA 2012, *supra* note 23.

3.3 Home purchase loan pricing

Manufactured-home borrowers typically pay higher interest rates for their loans than site-built borrowers. One illustration of this difference is the greater share of manufactured-housing loans that are classified as higher-priced mortgage loans (HPMLs) compared with site-built mortgage loans. HPMLs are dwelling-secured loans with annual percentage rates (APRs) at least 150 basis points (or 350 basis points for subordinate liens) over the applicable average prime offer rate (APOR).[65] The HPML definition was developed as a potential way to identify a set of loans that might be considered subprime. The HPML designation may trigger additional consumer protections, including rules regarding appraisals, escrows, and loans that qualify for the Bureau's safe harbor Qualified Mortgage (QM) designation.[66]

Of the first-lien loans reported under HMDA, about 68 percent of manufactured home purchase loans in 2012 were higher-priced, compared with three percent of purchase loans for site-built homes (Figure 7, top panel). The median rate spread over APOR for all purchase loans for manufactured homes (i.e., both HPML and non-HPML loans) in the 2012 HMDA data was 375 basis points.[67] Given that the average APOR for a fixed rate, 20-year loan in 2012 was 3.04 percent, a typical manufactured-housing loan in that year might have had an interest rate of 6.79 percent.

Even among the set of HPMLs, manufactured-home loans tend to have higher rates: APRs on higher-priced manufactured housing purchase loans averaged 570 basis points greater than APOR, whereas APRs on higher-priced site-built purchase loans averaged only 230 basis points greater than APOR.

---

[65] APOR is computed weekly using data from the Freddie Mac Primary Mortgage Market Survey. Fed. Fin. Inst. Examination Council (FFIEC), Rate Spread Calculator, *available at* https://www.ffiec.gov/ratespread/newcalc.aspx As described by the FFIEC, APOR is an estimate of APRs offered on prime mortgage loans with a given set of characteristics (for example, lock-in date and fixed or adjustable rate).

[66] *See infra* Appendix A for more details regarding these and selected other Bureau's consumer protection rules that affect dwelling-secured loans in the Appendix.

[67] Note that currently creditors report spread over APOR only for HPMLs. Since the vast majority of site-built loans are not HPMLs, it is impossible to compute the median APR over APOR spread for site-built loans using HMDA data. Similarly, it is impossible to compute the average APR over APOR spread for both site-built and manufactured housing loans. In 2014, the Bureau proposed changes to HMDA that would, among other things, allow researchers to analyze the mortgage market, and the manufactured housing segment of that market, more thoroughly. These changes include requiring creditors to report the APR over APOR spread on all loans, a field that would indicate whether a loan is chattel or real property, and points and fees.

FIGURE 7: HIGHER-PRICED AND HOEPA HIGH-COST LOANS, SHARE OF PURCHASE LOANS ORIGINATED BY HOUSING TYPE[68]

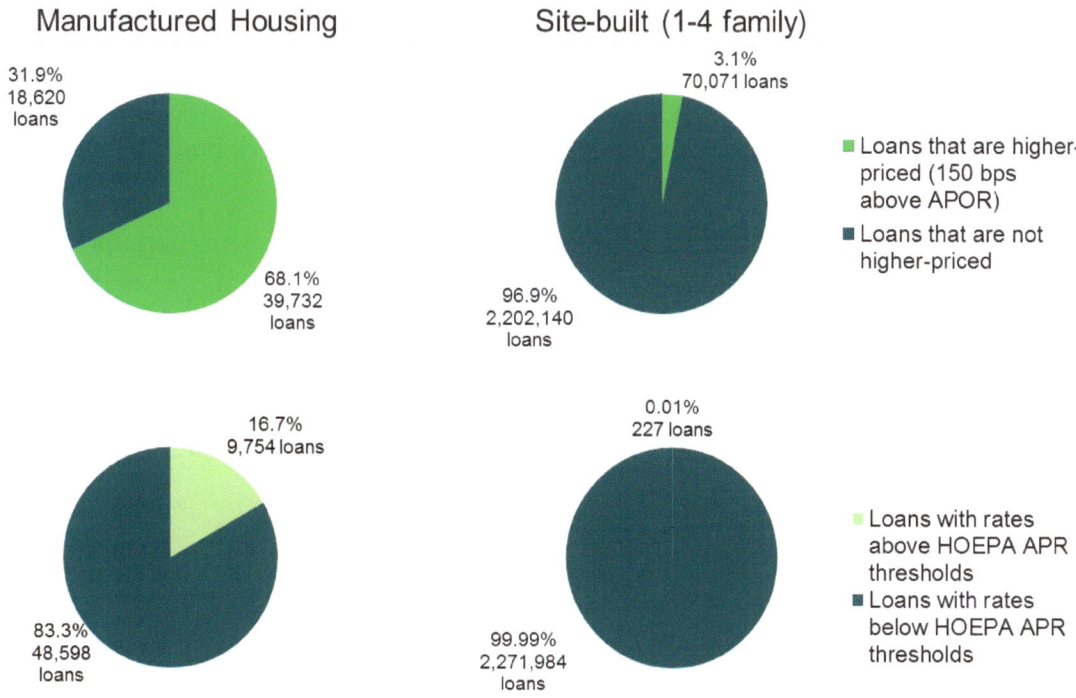

Loans for manufactured homes are also more likely to be classified as "high-cost" loans, as defined by the Homeownership and Equity Protection Act (HOEPA). High-cost loans (or "HOEPA loans") are those with an APR or points and fees that exceed certain thresholds. HOEPA provides certain protections to consumers that take out high-cost loans, including additional disclosures, home ownership counseling, and restrictions on certain loan contract terms. The first threshold is based on the loan's APR and is set at 650 basis points above APOR for all first-liens and 850 basis points for junior liens as well as for first-lien personal-property loans for less than $50,000. The second threshold is based on points and fees and, in general, is five percent of the loan amount, with different thresholds for loans under $50,000.

The Bureau analyzed 2012 HMDA data to compare first-lien manufactured-home and site-built loans that may be considered HOEPA loans. The current HOEPA thresholds described above did not take effect until 2013, so this analysis classified loans originated in 2012 as high-cost

---

[68] HMDA 2012, *supra* note 23.

mortgages as if the new Dodd-Frank APR thresholds had been in place in 2012.[69] In addition, because the HMDA data do not include points and fees, the analysis is restricted to loans with an interest rate that exceed HOEPA's APR threshold.[70]

Most loans with rates that exceed the HOEPA APR threshold in HMDA are for manufactured homes and, in particular, for home-purchase loans for manufactured housing. Of the roughly 10,600 first-lien home-purchase, refinance, or home improvement loans reported under HMDA with rates that exceed the HOEPA APR threshold, about 10,000 are for manufactured homes. Of these, nearly 9,800 are home-purchase loans for manufactured homes.[71]

In addition, the share of first-lien home-purchase loans for manufactured housing with interest rates that exceed the HOEPA APR threshold is considerably greater among those for amounts less than $50,000 even though the threshold for loans amount under $50,000 is 200 basis points higher than for larger loans. More specifically, considering only first-lien loans for the purchase of a manufactured home, about 21 percent of these loans for less than $50,000 have interest rates that exceeded the HOEPA APR threshold, compared with about 13 percent for larger loans, (amounts of at least $50,000).

As shown in the lower panel of Figure 7, HOEPA's additional consumer protections will likely apply to a much larger fraction of first-lien home-purchase loans for manufactured housing than for site-built housing. In particular, by these estimates, 0.2 percent of all home-purchase loans in the U.S. have an interest rate that exceeds the HOEPA APR threshold. This fraction is only

---

[69] *See infra* Appendix A for background information on the HOEPA rule and recent changes.

[70] In this analysis, we use "rate that exceeds the HOEPA APR threshold" as a shorthand to denote loans that have APRs in HMDA such that when the loans were made the spread between the APR and APOR is greater than 650 bps for loans over $50,000 and is greater than 850 bps for loans that are under $50,000. The analysis is further restricted to only loans secured by an owner-occupied, 1–4 family property and excludes loans taken out by a business.

[71] The HOEPA APR threshold for chattel loans under $50,000 is 850 bps over APOR. For the purposes of this analysis, we assume that all first-lien manufactured-housing loans in HMDA with loan amount of under $50,000 and APR over APOR spread of between 650 and 850 bps are chattel loans. Anecdotal and survey evidence supports this assumption. For example, based on evidence from various surveys, the Bureau previously assumed that 75 percent of manufactured-housing loans in HMDA under $50,000 are chattel loans; however, that proportion is likely to be higher for loans that have APR over APOR spread of over 650 bps. Assuming that none of the manufactured-housing loans in HMDA with loan amount of under $50,000 and with a spread between 650 and 850 bps are chattel loans leads to a higher number of manufactured-housing loans that have the spread over the threshold: approximately 15,500 instead of 10,000, but does not significantly change other findings in this subsection.

0.01 percent for site-built homes but nearly 17 percent for manufactured homes.[72] It is not possible from data currently reported through HMDA to assess the extent to which the greater share of manufactured housing loans that exceed the HOEPA APR thresholds compared with loans for site-built homes is generally attributable to differences in the credit profile of manufactured-home borrowers such as credit scores, debt-to-income ratios, loan-to-value or other such factors.

FIGURE 8: MANUFACTURED HOME PURCHASE LOANS ABOVE HOEPA HIGH-COST APR THRESHOLD, BY LOAN AMOUNT, BASED ON 2012 HMDA DATA[73]

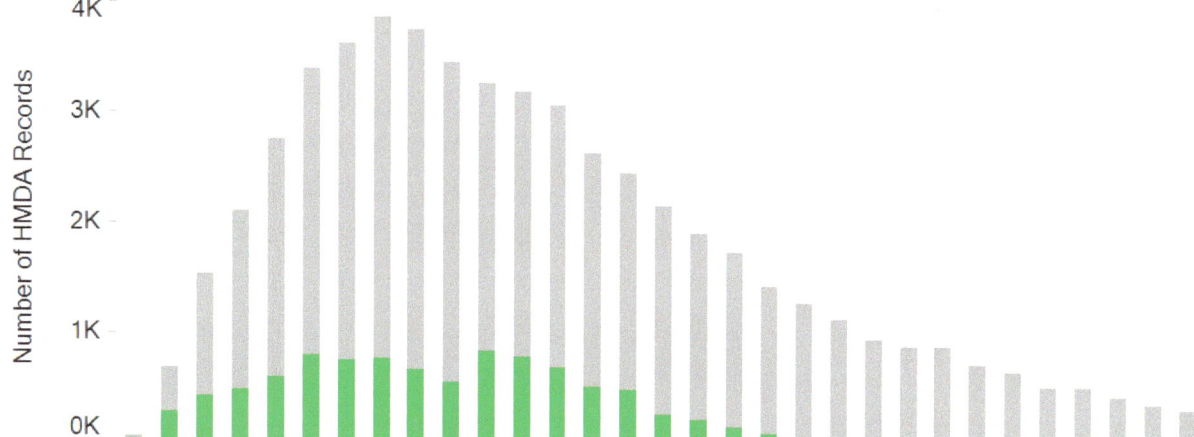

Based on HMDA data, the majority of these loans with APRs that exceed the HOEPA APR threshold for manufactured homes were originated by two creditors—the only creditors that originated more than 250 manufactured-home loans for home-purchase in 2012 that have rates that exceed the HOEPA APR threshold. These two creditors originated approximately 5,500 and

---

[72] The estimated share for manufactured-housing loans falls to about ten percent for all loans (i.e., home-purchase, refinance, and home improvement loans).

[73] HMDA 2012, *supra* note 23. Note that analysis is for first-lien home-purchase loans secured by a 1–4 family property, excludes loans to businesses, and considers only the APR threshold; not the points and fees threshold because points and fees are not reported in HMDA. The estimate also assumes all loans with APR spreads between 650 and 850 bps over APR are secured by personal property. Finally, it assumes no lender response to the enactment of the HOEPA final rule.

3,300 home-purchase loans for manufactured homes, respectively, with rates that exceed the HOEPA APR thresholds. Together, these originations account for roughly 91 percent of all home-purchase loans for manufactured homes in 2012 that have rates that exceed the HOEPA APR threshold. In contrast, these two creditors originated 38 percent of the home-purchase loans for manufactured homes in HMDA overall. There could be several reasons why the loans that these creditors made in 2012 were more likely to exceed the new HOEPA APR thresholds. For example, these creditors make a particularly large number of chattel loans. It is also possible that these creditors make manufactured-housing loans with differences in, for instance, credit scores, collateral, or other borrower characteristics that are not measured in HMDA.

On top of pricing differences between loans for manufactured housing compared with site-built homes, loan rates also differ between chattel and mortgage loans for manufactured homes. Borrowers with chattel financing typically pay higher prices than those with mortgage financing for a manufactured home. Proprietary data voluntarily provided to the Bureau by some manufactured home lenders do not show economically substantial differences in income, debt-to-income ratios, credit scores, and loan-to-value ratios between borrowers with chattel loans compared to those with mortgage loans. Thus pricing differences may stem, for example, from differences in collateral type or differences in other borrower characteristics that are not captured in these data. For the lenders in the sample utilized, loan amounts and points and fees tend to be about 40 to 50 percent lower for chattel loans, and APRs on chattel loans are about 150 basis points higher on average than for mortgages on manufactured homes.

The following example illustrates the relative prices of an HPML and a HOEPA loan for a manufactured home. Assume that a consumer purchases an average new multi-section manufactured home for $80,000, pays 20 percent down and takes out a 20-year fixed-rate loan for $64,000. The APOR on a 20-year fixed-rate loan is 3.36 percent as of August 11th 2014. The principal and interest payments for a $64,000 loan with this term, interest rate of 3.36 percent, and no points and fees would be $367 per month. In contrast, a second consumer's payments, for a 20-year, no points-and-fees loan with an interest rate of 4.87 percent – just over the HPML threshold of APOR plus 150 basis points – would be $418 per month. A third consumer's payments for a 20-year, no points-and-fees loan with an interest rate of 9.87 percent—just over the HOEPA APR threshold of APOR plus 650 basis points—would be $612 per month. See Table 6 below for an illustration of the preceding example.

TABLE 6: EXAMPLE LOAN CHARACTERISTICS AND MONTLY PAYMENTS. POINTS AND FEES ARE NOT INCLUDED IN THE TABLE OR THE ANALYSIS.

	Consumer 1: Loan at APOR	Consumer 2: Loan at HPML APR	Consumer 3: Loan at the HOEPA high-cost APR
Manufactured home price	$80,000	$80,000	$80,000
20-year fixed-rate loan at 80% loan-to-value	$64,000	$64,000	$64,000
Rate	3.36%	4.87%	9.87%
Percentage points above APOR	0%	1.50%	6.50%
Monthly payment	**$367**	**$418**	**$618**

3.4 Secondary market for manufactured-housing loans in 2014

Due to the limited secondary market for both manufactured-home chattel and mortgage loans, over 70 percent of manufactured-home loans in HMDA are held in portfolio, compared with about 16 percent of mortgages for site-built homes.[74] The secondary market for manufactured-housing loans differs markedly from that for site-built. For example, the GSEs purchase a substantial share of site-built loans originated in any given year but only a tiny fraction of manufactured-housing loans, at least in part because their involvement is limited to loans secured by real property.

---

[74] HMDA 2012, *supra* note 23. The analysis is restricted to only loans secured by an owner-occupied, 1–4 family property and excludes loans taken out by a business.

The vast majority of HMDA-reported manufactured-housing loans held in portfolio were higher-priced (82 percent), and their average loan amount was about half that of loans sold on the secondary market ($52,600 and $104,500, respectively). It is likely that most of the loans held in portfolio are chattel loans, for which secondary market demand has been depressed over the last decade.

Though the GSEs play a much smaller role in the secondary market for manufactured-housing loans than in the market for site-built loans, government programs exist to facilitate manufactured housing lending. 17 percent of manufactured-housing loans for home purchase in 2012 were guaranteed by Ginnie Mae for sale in the secondary market, eligible by virtue of origination under Federal Housing Administration (FHA), Department of Veterans Affairs (VA) or the U.S. Department of Agriculture's Rural Development (RD) lending programs.[75]

Recognizing the "prolonged downturn" in the manufactured home industry, Congress passed the FHA Manufactured housing loan Modernization Act in 2006.[76] The law mandated changes to FHA's Title I program, which covers home-only (chattel) purchase loans for manufactured housing, to remove impediments to Ginnie Mae securitization of such loans. FHA-guaranteed loans constituted about a fifth of manufactured-housing loans for home purchase in 2012, whereas VA and RD loans together amounted to less than five percent. The FHA has two programs for manufactured home purchase lending, one each for real and personal property-secured lending. The credit requirements for FHA chattel borrowers are less stringent than for mortgages, though lenders are required to retain more credit risk under the Title I chattel program, as shown in Table 7 below. Accordingly, Ginnie Mae now operates a home-only (FHA Title I) chattel loan guarantee program. Only one issuer was active in the space as of early 2014, largely due to a lack of investor demand. In 2012 Ginnie Mae was the most active secondary market participant for all manufactured-housing loans, although almost exclusively through their single-family mortgage-backed securities program.

---

[75] HMDA 2012, *supra* note 23.
[76] Comm. on Fin. Servs., Report on H.R. 2139, FHA Manufactured Housing Loan Modernization Act,, H.R. Rep. No. 110-206, (2007).

FHA Title I	FHA Title II
Personal property	Real estate, permanent foundation
Land only, land/home, or home only; site can be leased	Unit and land only; site must be owned and titled as real estate
Loan limits: MH only: $69,678 Lot only: $23,226 Combination: $92,904	FHA site-built limits apply: $271,050-$625,500 by area
5% down if credit score is 500+ 10% down if credit score is <500	Like FHA site-built requirements: 3.5% down Or 10% if credit score is <580
FHA insures maximum 90% of loan	Insures all of loan loss

3.5   Production of manufactured housing

As discussed above, the manufactured housing secondary market experienced a crisis in the early 2000s. The last decade has not seen a recovery in manufactured home production and retail industries. Instead, manufacturers have gone out of business or consolidated: compared to approximately 88 manufactured housing producers in the U.S. in 2002, around half that many are active in the space today. Some of this consolidation is due to large national manufacturers' purchases of failing manufacturers but a fragmented market with dozens of smaller regional manufacturers remains today. Production remains 15 percent lower than the overall peak in 1998 when production exceeded 373,000 units before it declined through the 2000s.[78] Since 2009, however, shipments have showed slight but steady gains. Early data from 2014 indicate year-over-year growth continues—in the first six months of 2014, shipments were up 5.6 percent over the same period in 2013.

---

[77] Federal Housing Administration.
[78] MH Census, *supra* note 3.

The largest three manufacturers held almost 70 percent market share of new manufactured housing production as of the end of 2013. Clayton Homes, a subsidiary of Berkshire Hathaway, has been the largest manufacturer by market share for over a decade, with home production share of 45 percent as of the end of 2013.[79] Other large national and regional manufacturers include Cavco Industries, Champion Home Builders, Legacy Housing, and Skyline Corporation. Currently the producers of manufactured homes in the U.S. operate 125 production line sites located across the country.[80] Outside of the top three manufacturers, none of the remaining corporations hold market share greater than five percent, and they average just over one production line each.[81]

FIGURE 9: SHIPMENTS OF NEW MANUFACTURED HOMES. MONTHLY, SEASONALLY ADJUSTED, JANUARY 2009-JUNE 2014[82]

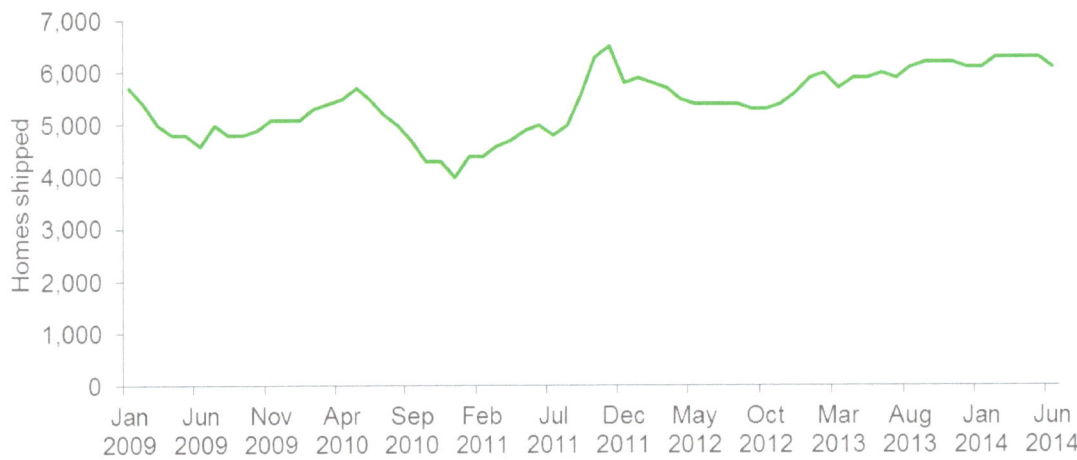

3.6 Retail

The manufactured housing retail industry consists of dealerships which sell new and used manufactured homes to consumers through retail storefronts. The retailer segment is highly fragmented and new entrants are rare. Manufactured-housing retailers are typically small,

---

[79] MHI and Institute for Building Technology and Safety (IBTS), Inc., *supra* note 40.

[80] *Id.*

[81] *Id.*

[82] MH Census, *supra* note 3.

independent businesses with one or several locations, though few have more than ten sales centers. In addition to selling through a network of independent retailers, the largest few manufacturers maintain company-owned networks of stores, ranging from a few regional outlets to a nationwide presence of hundreds. Even among retailers within a manufacturer's owned or affiliated network, it is far more common for a retailer to carry homes from multiple lines than to exclusively sell one manufacturer's models. In general, retailers utilize a floor plan line of credit to purchase inventory. The wholesale lender is paid back with the proceeds from the sale, either paid in cash by the buyer or financed and paid by the creditor, and the retailer generates profit on the home sale's margin. Retailers are typically obligated to oversee the transport and proper installation of the home on site after it is built and transported.

A consumer's visit to a manufactured housing retailer may resemble a car-buying experience more than a typical site-built home-buying experience in that the consumer may make a purchase decision in a sales lot displaying model new homes alongside pre-owned homes for sale. Moreover, as with auto financing, a consumer choosing to finance the purchase of a manufactured home often submits home loan applications while shopping at the retailer.

Manufactured-housing buyers seeking financing at a retailer may be constrained by particular relationships between retailers and home lenders. Most large national chattel lenders require independent retailers to enter into non-exclusive contractual agreements in order for the retailers' customers to be able to access the lender's financing; these lenders will not offer loans to consumers shopping outside of their network of partner retailers. In order for a consumer to purchase a home from a particular retailer with financing from a particular lender, the retailer and lender must first agree to conduct business together. If a particular lender and retailer do not have an agreement, a consumer must try to obtain financing from a different local or national lender willing to finance purchases from that retailer or purchase a home from a retailer approved by the lender. Smaller regional or local lenders which engage in chattel lending for manufactured homes on a more limited basis may not require specific agreements.

The prevalence of retailer-lender contractual agreements arose out of the particular incentive structure involved with manufactured housing sales and financing. The funding model allows a retailer to be paid for the home sale before the installation is completed. Agreements with retailers give lenders leverage during this period, decreasing the risk that quality issues in the completion of the installation cause a consumer to walk away from a home. Additionally, at least one national lender's retailer agreement obliges retailers to periodically sell homes owned by the lender on consignment. According to a Government Accountability Office report, having a good network of retailers to resell manufactured homes contributes to higher lender recovery rates on foreclosed homes; a strong recovery program could net a 50 percent recovery rate.[83] In general, a retailer's goal of selling homes provides incentives for the retailer to partner with lenders to offer financing options to potential home buyers. However, a retailer may choose not to partner with a certain lender if the retailer believes its market does not fit the lender's risk profile, or if terms of the contract are deemed disagreeable.

3.7 Manufactured home communities

There are about 60,000 land-lease manufactured home communities in the US.[84] Manufactured-home communities lease plots of land to owners or renters of manufactured housing. Residents of manufactured-home communities most often have equity in their home but pay monthly ground rent for the home's site and fees for common services. The community business model is built around revenue generation from ground rents, though community operators may also sell or rent new or pre-owned homes directly to consumers.

The industry of manufactured-home community owners is highly fragmented and populated with many single-site operators. The largest land-lease community owners include publicly- and privately-held Real Estate Investment Trusts (REITs) and property investment firms as well as specialty institutional investors. The largest publicly-held portfolio of manufactured-home communities is owned by Equity LifeStyle Properties, a Chicago-based REIT, and consists of 201 community properties with over 70,000 manufactured-home and park model home sites.[85]

The industry has been marked in recent years by consolidation, as growth has been focused on existing communities; investors have pursued acquisitions of both single-site operators and larger portfolios of manufactured-home community assets. One large community operator with over 50,000 sites in 161 communities noted in 2014 that the average length of time that a home resides in their communities is 40 years, while the average resident tenure is 13 years, indicating

---

[83] GAO, *supra* note 41.

[84] Housing Assistance Council, *Preserving Affordable Manufactured Home Communities in Rural America: A Case Study,* March 2011, *available at* http://www.ruralhome.org/storage/documents/rcbi_manufactured.pdf.

[85] *See* Equity LifeStyles Properties, *2014Q2 Investor Presentation*, *available at* http://phx.corporate-ir.net/phoenix.zhtml?c=105322&p=irol-presentations.

that multiple owners cycle through the same home within such communities.[86] Some communities support community occupancy by offering in-house lending to prospective manufactured-home buyers, either through the community's line of credit or a partner lending institution. In other cases, a consumer may purchase a home and select a community separately. Lot size availability in part determines home choice when a manufactured-home owner wishes to place a new home or move a pre-owned home to a community site.

In various manufactured-home communities around the country, residents have collectively purchased land from former operators in order to establish resident-owned communities (ROCs). This model was pioneered by groups with non-profit organization support in New Hampshire, where a fifth of communities are now resident-owned.[87] ROCs operate within a co-op shared equity model. In this model, a co-op member pays a monthly fee for the cost of shared services, utilities, or amenities plus their share of the cost of debt servicing for the initial land purchase. Generally, if and when individual co-op members decide to sell their property, they receive back their equity in the land with no appreciation.

---

[86] *See* Sun Communities, Inc., *June 2014 Investor Presentation, available at* http://www.suncommunities.com/Investors.aspx.
[87] *See* ROC USA, *Background, available at* http://www.rocusa.org/about-us/background/default.aspx.

4. Conclusion

This white paper provides background on manufactured housing and families that live in manufactured homes and highlights differences between manufactured housing and site-built homes along these dimensions. Among the most important of these differences is their legal treatment. Site-built homes are nearly always titled as real estate property, whereas many manufactured homes may be titled as either real estate property or personal property (chattel), even if the manufactured-home owner owns the land the home is sited on. Chattel loans may close more quickly than or have lower upfront costs than loans secured by real property, but chattel loans tend to have higher interest rates and provide borrowers with lesser consumer protections than mortgages secured by real property.

The findings also indicate the potential importance of manufactured housing as a source of affordable housing for some consumers. Families that live in manufactured-homes, for example, tend to have lower income and net worth than families in site-built homes, and manufactured homes are generally less expensive than site-built homes. Families in rural areas are also relatively more likely to live in manufactured homes, and in some counties as much as one-third or more of homes are manufactured homes.

This white paper brings together data and information on manufactured housing from a variety of sources to develop a more-complete and current picture of manufactured housing. The Bureau will continue to analyze facets of manufactured housing markets and to consider new data that may help to further fill in this picture. The relative scarcity of data on manufactured housing compared with data available on site-built housing and mortgage finance in general remains a challenge for research related to manufactured housing. This gap in data availability may begin to narrow, however, in the coming years. The Bureau is considering, for example, adding a field to the HMDA data that would indicate whether a manufactured-housing loan is secured by real or personal property. Further, additional sets of five-year estimates from the ACS will provide larger sample sizes that may support in-depth analyses. The Bureau hopes that this white paper and analysis of additional data will encourage others to build greater knowledge of the manufactured housing market, the consumers in that market, and the differences between the site-built and manufactured housing markets as well.

APPENDIX A:

Recent changes to consumer financial protection laws and their potential impact on manufactured housing

Transactions involving manufactured housing have long been covered by several laws designed to protect consumers in financial transactions. However, title XIV of the Dodd-Frank Act recently amended existing laws to expand consumer protections in mortgage (both land and home and chattel) transactions. These expanded protections were implemented by the CFPB in a series of rules which took effect in January 2014. This appendix looks at some of the major provisions of the CFPB's rules and their potential impact on manufactured-housing loans.

Homeownership and Equity Protection Act (HOEPA)

In 1994 the Home Ownership and Equity Protection Act (HOEPA) was enacted as part of the Truth in Lending Act (TILA) to provide certain protections to consumers in high-cost transactions involving their homes, including manufactured homes.[88] Regulation Z implements HOEPA and TILA. A mortgage is subject to HOEPA if it is a high-cost mortgage (commonly called a "HOEPA loan") because of a comparatively high interest rate or points and fees. Among

---

[88] TILA's Regulation Z's coverage generally extends to loans secured by manufactured homes regardless of whether the homes are titled as personal or real property. See, e.g., 15 USC 164x (w), "dwelling means a residential structure or a mobile home…"; see also 12 CFR part 1026, Supp. I, paragraph 2(a)(17),

other requirements for a HOEPA loan, the creditor must provide additional disclosures to the consumer, and certain loan terms such as negative amortization, and rate increases following default are restricted.

Prior to the enactment of the Dodd-Frank Act, HOEPA did not apply to loans for home purchase.[89] In Dodd-Frank, Congress extended HOEPA to home purchase loans and amended HOEPA's APR triggers so as generally to cover first liens with an APR greater than APOR plus 650 basis points and junior liens with an APR greater than APOR plus 850 basis points.[90] Dodd-Frank also lowered the points and fees triggers to five percent for most mortgages, with some adjustment for smaller loan amounts as discussed below.[91] Together, the Dodd-Frank changes likely increased the share of manufactured-home loans that are classified as HOEPA loans substantially.[92] Congress also added new protections for consumers taking out HOEPA loans, including a requirement for pre-loan housing counseling.

Recognizing that loans for smaller amounts are more costly to originate (in percentage terms), Congress made certain adjustments to HOEPA's triggers. Dodd-Frank adjusted the HOEPA points and fees threshold for loans less than $20,000. As amended, HOEPA establishes a points and fees threshold of the lesser of eight percent of the total transaction amount or $1,000. Congress also recognized that smaller chattel loans require a higher rate-spread threshold. For personal property loans under $50,000, HOEPA applies if the loans have an APR greater than APOR plus 850 basis points (instead of APOR plus 650 basis points). The vast majority of these personal property loans are for manufactured homes.

In their comments during the HOEPA rulemaking process, some industry commenters stated that these adjusted HOEPA thresholds were still too low. They stated that they would not make HOEPA loans and therefore consumers would experience reduced access to credit for manufactured-home loans. Some large manufactured-housing creditors urged the Bureau to establish an APR threshold of APOR plus 1,000 or 1,200 basis points. Such a threshold would

---

[89] HOEPA also did not apply to open-end home-secured transactions before the Dodd-Frank Act expansion.

[90] Prior to Dodd-Frank, a first lien loan was covered if its APR exceeded the yield on comparable Treasury securities by more than 800 basis points (or by more than 1000 basis points for subordinate lien loans).

[91] Prior to Dodd-Frank, the points and fees threshold was the greater of eight percent of the total loan amount, or a dollar figure adjusted annually for inflation. In 2013, the dollar figure was $625.

[92] Dodd-Frank also added a pre-payment penalty trigger. Under the Dodd-Frank amendments a loan is covered by HOEPA if the loan contains a penalty for prepaying the loan in whole or in part, even if the loan's APR or points and fees do not exceed the thresholds discussed above.

mean that a 20-year fixed-rate loan is covered by HOEPA if its APR is about 13.4 to 15.4 percent, based on APOR as of August 11, 2014. The industry also suggested that the points and fees threshold should be restored to its pre-Dodd-Frank level at eight percent of the total loan amount. A few large manufactured-housing creditors argued that without such adjustments, roughly one-third to one-half of their manufactured housing would be classified as HOEPA loans based on the APR threshold, and about one-quarter to nearly one-half of these lenders' loans would be classified as HOEPA loans based on the points-and-fees test.

Notwithstanding these arguments, the Bureau decided to implement the statute as Congress had written it, rather than use its authority to make adjustments beyond those that Congress deemed appropriate. In part this was because of uncertainty as to whether, in fact, a substantial number of creditors would cease making manufactured-housing loans if those loans triggered HOEPA protections. Moreover, the Bureau reasoned that the manufactured housing borrowers being charged interest rates or upfront fees above the HOEPA thresholds are the very populations that HOEPA is designed to protect.

High-cost mortgages—those that exceed HOEPA's APR or points-and-fees thresholds—have historically represented a small share of loans for manufactured homes and for site-built homes. On average in the 2004–2011 HMDA data, about 0.2 percent of home-secured refinance and home-improvement loans (the types of mortgages covered by HOEPA prior to 2014) were classified as high-cost mortgages. This fraction had generally declined since 2004 and was 0.06 percent in the 2011 HMDA data. The extension of HOEPA to home-purchase loans increased the share of all loans (i.e., home-purchase, refinance or home improvement loans) that are classified as HOEPA loans, but the resulting increase in the share of high-cost mortgages was much larger for manufactured-housing loans than for loans on site-built homes.

The Bureau's estimate of the share of loans with rates that exceed the HOEPA APR threshold is intended to be illustrative. Focusing on only loans that would be high-cost mortgages based on APR alone understates the fraction of loans that might be classified as high-cost mortgages, as some loans may have rates that do not exceed the HOEPA APR threshold but points and fees that exceed the HOEPA points and fees threshold. At the same time, the retrospective analysis included in section 3.3, "Home purchase loan pricing," above may be overly inclusive because it does not take into account a creditor's ability to structure a loan's interest rate and upfront costs in a way that does not reduce the loan's profitability but ensures that the loan is not classified as a high-cost mortgage. Similarly, the estimate does not account for the cases in which creditors may choose to reduce a loan's profitability simply to avoid making a high-cost mortgage loan. Specifically, a creditor that would have originated only a handful of HOEPA loans might prefer to restructure those loans, even at a reduced profit, to avoid HOEPA coverage altogether. Indeed, some large creditors report performing such a trade-off, effectively lowering some consumers' APRs so as not to exceed the threshold.

Finally, the Bureau is aware that a large manufactured-housing creditor, 21st Mortgage, recently indicated that it will stop originating loans for less than $20,000. According to the HMDA data, 21st Mortgage originated less than 1,500 of such loans in 2012, and there were only a handful of counties where more than 20 manufactured-housing loans for less than $20,000 were originated in 2012 and 21st Mortgage originated the majority of manufactured-housing loans under $20,000.

Qualified Mortgage (QM) and Ability-to-Repay (ATR)

In 2010, the Dodd-Frank Act amended TILA to require that, before making a residential mortgage, a creditor must make a "reasonable and good faith determination based on verified and documented information that, at the time the loan is consummated, the consumer has a reasonable ability to repay the loan." [93] The Act establishes a private cause of action if a creditor violates this ability-to-repay requirement. The ability-to-repay requirement sets forth certain requirements for loans secured by dwellings, including that the creditor verify the consumer's ability to repay the loan. For a loan that meets the criteria for a qualified mortgage ("QM"), the creditor is presumed to have complied with the ATR requirement. The QM criteria include, among other things, a three percent limit on points and fees, with higher points and fees limits for loans of $100,000 or less. Under the CFPB's implementing regulations, QMs with APRs that do not exceed APOR by 150 basis points or more provide a conclusive presumption of compliance with the ability-to-repay rules, and the creditor enjoys a safe harbor from potential

---

[93] In 2008, the Federal Reserve Board issued amendments to Regulation Z which required a creditor to make an ability to repay determination, but this requirement only applied to loans deemed to be "higher-priced" mortgages— i.e., loans with APRs that exceeded APOR by 150 basis points (or 350 basis points for subordinate liens). Under the Federal Reserve Board's rules, creditors could obtain a rebuttable presumption of compliance with the ability to repay requirement if they met the rule's criteria for the presumption. These rules applied to manufactured-housing loans that met the "higher-priced" APR trigger. In 2010, Dodd-Frank essentially extended the ability to repay requirement to all mortgage loans, not just higher-priced mortgage loans, effective in January 2014 when the CFPB's implementing regulations took effect.

ATR liability. For QMs with rate-spreads that exceed APOR by 150 basis points or more, the presumption is subject to rebuttal under narrowly-defined criteria (rebuttable presumption QM).[94]

Note that small creditors are eligible to originate QMs with more flexible criteria. For instance, the rate spread threshold for a safe harbor small creditor QM is 350 basis points. Small creditors are defined as creditors that originated 500 or fewer first lien mortgages in the previous year and have an asset size of less than two billion dollars.

The previous section noted that some manufactured-home loans are likely to be covered by HOEPA's new APR threshold of more than 650 basis points over the applicable APOR. Note that a loan with a rate spread that exceeds HOEPA's threshold may still be a QM provided that all of the QM criteria are met. However, such a loan will also exceed the threshold for the QM safe harbor (whether 150 or 350 basis points, depending on whether the creditor is small) and thus will be a rebuttable presumption QM. For manufactured-housing loans that trigger HOEPA due to points and fees exceeding the HOEPA thresholds, such loans would exceed the three percent points and fees limit for QMs and thus would be non-QM loans.

To the extent manufactured-housing loans are subject to HOEPA, then, they also necessarily are either rebuttable presumption QMs or non-QMs, depending on whether they come under HOEPA coverage via the APR test or the points-and-fees test. However, creditors have some degree of flexibility to trade off as between points and fees and interest rates (and thus APRs). Accordingly, they may be able to control for which of these two results they encounter; presumably, assuming creditors prefer rebuttable presumption QMs to non-QMs, manufactured-housing creditors may shift their overall loan pricing out of points and fees and into interest rates to the extent feasible.

---

[94] For subordinate lien loans, the rate spread for a safe harbor QM is 350 basis points. Note that for loans that are not qualified mortgages, there is no presumption of compliance with the ability-to-repay requirement. If a consumer can prove that a creditor failed to comply with the ability-to-repay requirement, the consumer may be able to recover damages provided for in TILA.

Loan-Originator Compensation

In recent years, regulators and lawmakers have imposed a number of new requirements concerning loan originators' licensing and registration, training, screening, and compensation practices. In 2010, the Dodd-Frank Act adopted new requirements that built on some of these earlier initiatives. In defining loan originators who would be subject to the requirements, Congress provided that an employee of a manufactured home retailer is not a loan originator if the employee does not take applications and does not advise about, offer, or negotiate loan terms. The Bureau issued regulations to implement the new Dodd-Frank Act requirements in January 2013 and issued further amendments in September 2013 (the Bureau's Loan Originator Rule). The regulations expand upon and refine earlier regulations adopted by the Federal Reserve Board (that became effective in April 2011 and were restated by the Bureau in December 2011) to restrict certain compensation practices. The regulations also implement Dodd-Frank Act requirements concerning loan originator qualifications that build upon existing requirements under the Secure and Fair Enforcement for Mortgage Licensing Act of 2008 (SAFE Act).

The Loan Originator Rule limits creditors' ability to pay loan originators (LOs) compensation that is based on the terms of the loan. The Bureau implemented Congress's definition of loan originator, including the provision specifically relating to employees of manufactured home retailers noted above. The Bureau has clarified the instances when a manufactured-housing retailer's employees would not be considered individual loan originators. A manufactured-housing retailer's employees are not considered loan originators if they do not take a consumer credit application, offer or negotiate credit terms, or advise a consumer on credit terms. They are considered loan originators if they engage in loan originator activities such as referring consumers to a particular creditor, filling out a consumer's loan application, or inputting a consumer's information into an online loan application.

Advising consumers about a loan application and referring consumers to a creditor are LO activities, and many manufactured-housing retailers do not want to incur the cost of becoming a licensed LO. Thus, retailers report that, instead of referring a consumer to a particular creditor or two, they currently do not advise consumers about which creditors are most likely to accept their applications. As a result, industry participants have stated that consumers are applying to more creditors than before. While this is not per se contrary to the purposes of the rule – in fact, increased consumer shopping generally is a positive development – this dynamic also results in consumers in the current credit environment applying to creditors who are almost certain to reject their applications. For example, a consumer with a credit score of 550 may apply to a creditor that originates loans only to consumers with credit scores over 680. In turn, this results in more volume of applications for creditors, all of which need to be processed in a timely manner and at least some of which necessarily will be rejected. It follows that two of the effects of the Bureau's Loan Originator rule is a small cost increase to creditors that would have to spend more employee time screening applications and an increase in the rejection rates of consumers' applications due to consumers submitting more applications.

The classification of some manufactured-housing retailer activities as loan originator activities provides consumer protection for homebuyers in what may be a high-pressure sales environment. As a result of the Loan Originator Rule and state SAFE Act provisions, consumers who purchase their dwellings through manufactured-housing retailers no longer face pressure (from compliant retailers) to finance their purchase through a particular creditor; rather, consumers are more likely to shop and compare credit offers. The Loan Originator Rule enables consumers to know that the retailer from whom they purchase a manufactured home does not steer them to a particular creditor or mishandle their application. Consumers can trust that a retailer who advises them on specific credit terms is qualified and licensed to do so.

Higher-Priced Appraisals

The Dodd-Frank Act made amendments to TILA to impose special appraisal requirements for certain higher-priced mortgages that do not meet the Bureau's definition of QM. Dodd-Frank requires an in-person appraisal for properties securing higher-priced mortgage loans. The Bureau and five other Agencies authorized to implement this requirement recently finalized a supplemental proposal that addressed issues related to manufactured housing.[95] The underlying concern was that many of the traditional appraisal methods would not be applicable or are not currently practiced in the manufactured housing market, especially for chattel transactions. The Bureau and the other Agencies adopted a tailored approach to the appraisal requirement for manufactured homes, with requirements that depend on the type of transaction (specifically, new real estate, used real estate, new chattel, and used chattel transactions), ensuring a

---

[95] 78 Fed. Reg. 78520 (Dec. 26, 2013).

smoother transition to the new regime. For most of these transactions, the rule is not going to become effective until 2015. There is also a smaller-dollar loan exemption in this rule.

This rule is designed to give borrowers vital information about their mortgage: the value of the home (including the land, where applicable). The rule exempts transactions secured by a new manufactured home and land from the requirement that the appraisal include a physical inspection of the interior of the property. Transactions secured solely by a manufactured home and not land will be exempt from the appraisal requirement if the creditor gives the consumer one of three types of information about the home's value. Given these exemptions, the smaller-dollar exemption, and the exemption for QM loans (both safe harbor and rebuttable presumption), this rule is unlikely to be burdensome to comply with.

Higher-Priced Escrows

In 2008, the Federal Reserve Board issued amendments to Regulation Z which required a creditor to establish an escrow account for any higher-priced loan secured by a first lien on a principal dwelling.[96] The Dodd-Frank Act made two major amendments to TILA with regards to escrow requirements for higher-priced loans. First, the Dodd-Frank Act required that the escrow account to be established for five years instead of one. Second, the Dodd-Frank Act authorized the Bureau to provide an exemption for small rural creditors.[97] The Bureau defined small creditors as for the purposes of QM designation (see above), while rural was defined as a creditor that makes more than half of its loans in rural or underserved areas.[98]

An escrow account provides borrowers protection from sudden shocks from tax and home insurance payments. The Bureau's rule extends that protection from one year to five while reducing access to credit concerns created by this requirement in rural or underserved areas.[99] Since most of manufactured housing loans are HPMLs, the Federal Reserve Board's rule likely

---

[96] 73 Fed. Reg. 44522 (July 30, 2008).

[97] Dodd-Frank Wall Street Reform and Consumer Protection Act, Pub. L. No. 111-203, § 1461 – 1462, 124 Stat. 1376 (2010).

[98] *See* Paul Mondor, Bureau of Consumer Fin. Prot., *Final list of rural and underserved counties for use in 2014*, CFPB Blog, *available at* http://www.consumerfinance.gov/blog/final-list-of-rural-and-underserved-counties-for-use-in-2014/ for the list of counties that were defined as rural or underserved for 2014.

[99] 78 Fed. Reg. 4726 (Jan. 22 2013).

imposed its requirements on most manufactured housing creditors. However, the Bureau's rule provided some relief for small manufactured housing creditors predominantly operating in rural or underserved areas. The Bureau believes that extending the escrow account protection from one year to five was not burdensome for the remaining creditors.

www.ingramcontent.com/pod-product-compliance
Lightning Source LLC
Chambersburg PA
CBHW050813180526
45159CB00004B/1650

* 9 7 8 1 5 0 6 1 3 1 7 0 2 *